POEMS FOR SUMMER

Selected by
Robert Hull

Illustrated by
Annabel Spenceley

Poems for Summer

Also available:

Poems for Autumn
Poems for Spring
Poems for Winter

Editor: Catherine Ellis
Designer: Ross George

First published in 1990 by
Wayland (Publishers) Ltd
61 Western Road, Hove
East Sussex BN3 1JD, England

© Copyright 1990 Wayland
(Publishers) Ltd

British Library Cataloguing in Publication Data

Poems for summer.
1. Children's poetry in English.
Special subjects:
Seasons – Anthologies
I. Hull, Robert II. Spenceley,
Annabel III. Series
821.008033
HARDBACK ISBN 1-85210-980-7
PAPERBACK ISBN 0-7502-0549-0

Picture Acknowledgements

The publishers wish to thank the following for allowing their illustrations to be reproduced in this book: Bruce Coleman 5 (Hans Reinhard), 10 (Jane Burton), 29 (Dick J. C. Klees), 31 (Hans Reinhard), 32 (George McCarthy); Eye Ubiquitous 6; Sally and Richard Greenhill 34, 36; the Hutchison Library 19; Frank Lane Picture Agency 20; Christine Osborne 15; ZEFA cover, 9, 12, 16, 23, 26, 41, 42, 45.

Typeset by Nicola Taylor, Wayland
Printed in Italy by G. Canale & C.S.p.A., Turin. Bound in France by A.G.M.

Acknowledgements

For permission to reprint copyright material the publishers gratefully acknowledge the following: Penguin Books Ltd for 'Sticky Licky' from *Smile Please!* by Tony Bradman (Viking Kestrel 1987), copyright © Tony Bradman, 1987; Unwin Hyman Ltd for 'In the Mountains on a Summer Day' and 'Heat', extracts taken from *Chinese Poems* by Arthur Waley, copyright Unwin Hyman Ltd; in the UK Grafton Books, a division of the Collins Publishing Group, and in the USA by permission of Liveright Publishing Corporation for 'maggie and milly and molly and may' from *Complete Poems 1936-1962* by e. e. cummings; Angus and Robertson (UK) Ltd for 'A Song of Rain' reprinted from *Selected Verse of C. J. Dennis*; 'A Narrow Fellow in the Grass' reprinted by permission of the publishers and the Trustees of Amherst College from *The Poems of Emily Dickinson*, edited by Thomas H. Johnson, Cambridge, Mass.: The Belknap Press of Harvard University Press; New Directions Publishing Corporation for 'Fortune' from *A Coney Island of the Mind* by Lawrence Ferlinghetti, copyright © 1958 by Lawrence Ferlinghetti. World rights granted; John Fuller for 'Bilberry Flan'; Rebecca Gaskell for 'Froglet'; Doubleday, a division of Bantam, Doubleday. Dell Publishing Group, Inc. for excerpts from *An Introduction to Haiku* by Harold G. Henderson, copyright © 1958 by Harold G. Henderson; Olwyn Hughes for 'Fantails' from *The Cat and the Cuckoo* by Ted Hughes, published by the Sunstone Press, © Ted Hughes 1987; Penguin Books Ltd for 'The Cabbage White Butterfly' from *Of Caterpillars, Cats and Cattle* by Elizabeth Jennings; Penguin USA for 'The Mirror' from *When We Were Very Young* by A. A. Milne; the James Reeves Estate for 'Green Grass' © James Reeves from *The Wandering Moon and Other Poems* (Puffin Books) by James Reeves; 'Summer Grass' from *Good Morning, America* by Carl Sandburg, © 1928 by Harcourt Brace Jovanovich Inc. and renewed 1956 by Carl Sandburg, reprinted by permission of the publisher; 'Sunning' from *Crickety Cricket! The Best Loved Poems of James S. Tippett*. Copyright 1933 by Harper and Row Publishers, Inc. Renewed 1973 by Martha Tippett. Reprinted by permission of HarperCollins Publishers.

While every effort has been made to trace the copyright holders, in some cases it has proved impossible. The publishers apologise for this apparent negligence.

Contents

Introduction

Do you get ice-cream up your nose? Poets do. Summer and ice-cream go together. Perhaps we like ice-cream even in the winter because it reminds us of being outside in the sun. Ice-cream is part of the real summer, being lazy and doing nothing, one of the best things you can ever do.

Li Po hung his cap on a tree in the mountains and wrote about doing nothing more than a thousand years ago in one of the poems in this book. What do cows ever do, Kaye Starbird asks. An old dog in another poem even *dreams* lazily!

If you're lucky, summer means lazy days by the sea, finding things the way maggie and milly and molly and may do – like the creature 'which raced sideways while blowing bubbles' or the 'stranded star'. Or you can stay at home and take a shower in the street, as in Lawrence Ferlinghetti's poem.

But summer can also mean burning heat and drought and longing for rain. It does in the Australian outback, in the poems about the drying up of the water-tank, and then the marvellous excitement when rain finally comes: 'It is raining – raining – raining!'

Summer feels as if it's for us. We can easily not notice the small creatures. The birds have gone quieter, the young ones lying low in the grass. We might see a small frog risking a few leaps down the lawn, or popping into the kitchen for a look around.

What is summer like in your poems?

Jigsaw Puddle

Sloshing my boat in the pavement puddle
I jiggle the sky above,
I fold the clouds in a sheep-like huddle,
I bobble the sun in the blue and white muddle –
And then I stand still –
Till the jigsaw puddle
Is smooth as a mirror again.

EMILY HEARN

The Vixen

Among the taller wood with ivy hung,
The old fox plays and dances round her young.
She snuffs and barks if any passes by
And swings her tail and turns prepared to fly.
The horseman hurries by, she bolts to see,
And turns agen, from danger never free.
If any stands she runs among the poles
And barks and snaps and drives them in their holes.
The shepherd sees them and the boy goes by
And gets a stick and progs the hole to try.
They get all still and lie in safety sure,
And out again when everything's secure,
And start and snap at blackbirds bouncing by
To fight and catch the great white butterfly.

JOHN CLARE

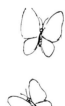

9

Fantails

Up on the roof the Fantail Pigeons dream
Of dollops of curled cream.

At every morning window their soft voices
Comfort all the bedrooms with caresses.

'Peace, peace, peace,' through the day
The Fantails hum and murmur and pray.

Like a dream, where resting angels crowded
The roof-slope, that has not quite faded.

When they clatter up, and veer, and soar in a ring
It's as if the house suddenly sang something.

The cats of the house, purring on lap and knee,
Dig their claws and scowl with jealousy.

TED HUGHES

Froglet

here

comes a
tenth-size
froglet

plink
plink
plink

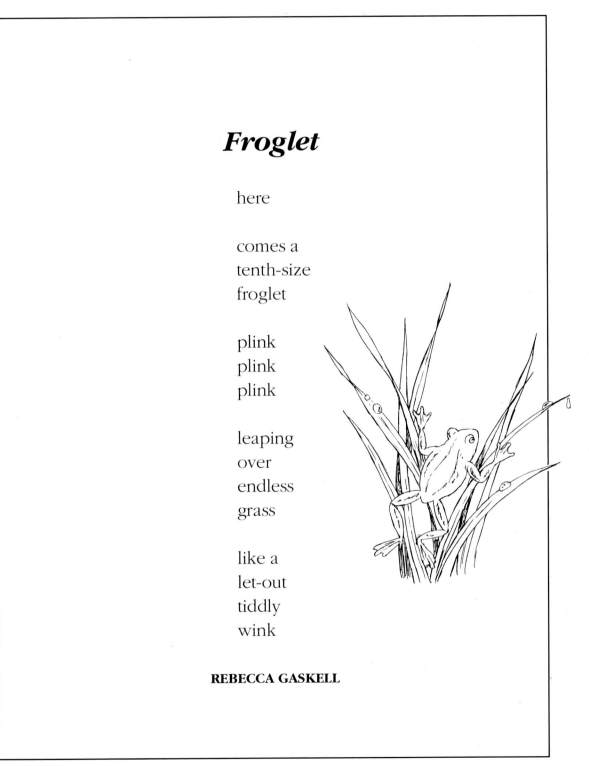

leaping
over
endless
grass

like a
let-out
tiddly
wink

REBECCA GASKELL

Green Grass

Green grass is all I hear
And grass is all I see
When through tall fields
  I wander
Swish-swishing to the knee.

Grass is short on the high heath
And long on the hillside.
There's where the rabbits burrow,
And here's where I hide.

The hillside is my castle,
Its walls are the tall grass;
Over them I peer and pry
To see the people pass.

Long and far I send my gaze
Over the valleys low.
There I can see but do not hear
The wagons lumbering slow.

Horseman, footman, shepherd, dog –
Here in my castle green
I see them move through vale and village,
I see but am not seen.

Green grasses whispering
  round me,
All in the summer fine,
Tell me your secrets, meadow
  grasses,
And I will tell you mine.

JAMES REEVES

14

Sunning

Old Dog lay in the summer sun
Much too lazy to rise and run.
He flapped an ear
At a buzzing fly.
He winked a half opened
Sleepy eye.
He scratched himself
On an itching spot,
As he dozed on the porch
Where the sun was hot.
He whimpered a bit
From force of habit
While he lazily dreamed
Of chasing a rabbit.
But Old Dog happily lay in the sun
Much too lazy to rise and run.

JAMES S. TIPPETT

Sugarfields

treetalk and windsong
are the language of my mother
her music does not leave me.

let me taste again the cane
the syrup of the earth
sugarfields were once my home.

I would lie down in the fields
and never get up again
(treetalk and windsong
are the language of my mother
sugarfields are my home)

the leaves go on whispering secrets
as the wind blows a tune in the grass
my mother's voice is in the fields
this music cannot leave me.

BARBARA MAHONE

19

The Cabbage White Butterfly

I look like a flower you could pick. My delicate wings
Flutter over the cabbages. I don't make
Any noise ever. I'm among silent things.
Also I easily break.

I have seen the nets in your hands. At first I thought
A cloud had come down but then I noticed you
With your large pink hand and arm. I was nearly caught
But fortunately I flew

Away in time, hid while you searched, then took
To the sky, was out of your reach. Like a nameless flower
I tried to appear. Can't you be happy to look?
Must you possess with your power?

ELIZABETH JENNINGS

The Way through the Woods

They shut the road through the woods
Seventy years ago.
Weather and rain have undone it again
And now you would never know
There was once a road through the woods
Before they planted the trees.
It is underneath the coppice and heath
And the thin anemones.
Only the keeper sees
That, where the ring-dove broods,
And the badgers roll at ease,
There was once a road through the woods.

Yet, if you enter the woods
Of a summer evening late,
When the night air cools on the trout-ringed pools
Where the otter whistles his mate,
(They fear not man in the woods
Because they see so few),
You will hear the beat of a horse's feet,
And the swish of a skirt in the dew,
Steadily cantering through
The misty solitudes,
As though they perfectly knew
The old lost road through the woods. . .
But there is no road through the woods!

RUDYARD KIPLING

Fortune

Fortune
            has its cookies to give out

which is a good thing

            since it's been a long time since

      that summer in Brooklyn
   when they closed off the street
         one hot day
         and the

                  FIREMEN

                        turned on their hoses

      and all the kids ran out in it

         in the middle of the street

and there were

            maybe a couple of dozen of us

                              out there

with the water squirting up

to the

sky

and all over
us

there was maybe only six of us
kids altogether
running around in our
barefeet and birthday

suits
and I remember Molly but then
the firemen stopped squirting their hoses
all of a sudden and went
back in
their firehouse
and
started playing pinochle again
just as if nothing
had ever
happened
While I remember Molly
looked at me and

ran in

because I guess really we were the only ones there

LAWRENCE FERLINGHETTI

25

The Mirror

Between the woods the afternoon
Is fallen in a golden swoon.
The sun looks down from quiet skies
To where a quiet water lies,
And silent trees stoop down to trees.
And there I saw a white swan make
Another white swan in the lake;
And, breast to breast, both motionless,
They waited for the wind's caress. . .
And all the water was at ease.

A. A. MILNE

Summer Grass

Summer grass aches and whispers.

It wants something; it calls and it sings; it pours
    out wishes to the overhead stars.

The rain hears; the rain answers; the rain is slow
    coming; the rain wets the face of the grass.

CARL SANDBURG

Bilberry Flan

Bilberry flan, bilberry flan:
Leave off eating where you began.

Bilberry tart, bilberry tart,
Large and sweet as a courtier's heart.

Bilberry jam, bilberry jam:
Sometimes we eat it with roast lamb.

Bilberry fool, bilberry fool:
Whip it with cream and let it cool.

Bilberry crumble, bilberry crumble:
Too-big mouthfuls make you mumble.

June to August we will pick
Bilberries until we're sick.

JOHN FULLER

A Narrow Fellow in the Grass

A narrow Fellow in the Grass
Occasionally rides –
You may have met Him – did you not
His notice sudden is –

The Grass divides as with a Comb –
A spotted shaft is seen –
And then it closes at your feet
And opens further on –

He likes a Boggy Acre
A Floor too cool for Corn –
Yet when a Boy, and Barefoot –
I more than once at Noon
Have passed, I thought, a Whip lash
Unbraiding in the Sun
When stooping to secure it
It wrinkled, and was gone –

Several of Nature's People
I know, and they know me –
I feel for them a transport
Of cordiality –

But never met this Fellow
Attended, or alone
Without a tighter breathing
And Zero at the Bone –

EMILY DICKINSON

maggie and milly and molly and may

maggie and milly and molly and may
went down to the beach (to play one day)

and maggie discovered a shell that sang
so sweetly she couldn't remember her troubles, and

milly befriended a stranded star
whose rays five languid fingers were;

and molly was chased by a horrible thing
which raced sideways while blowing bubbles: and

may came home with a smooth round stone
so small as a world and as large as alone.

For whatever we lose (like a you or a me)
it's always ourselves we find in the sea.

e. e. cummings

Sticky Licky

In the summer,
When it's sunny,
Eating ice-cream
Can be funny.

Ice-cream melts
And drips so fast
It's quite hard
To make it last.

It's so lovely,
Sweet and licky,
But when it drips,
You get sticky.

I get ice-cream
On my clothes,
In my hair
And up my nose.

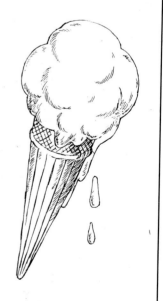

My dad says
I should eat less;
Ice-cream plus me
Equals – mess!

TONY BRADMAN

Our Corrugated Iron Tank

Our tank stood on a crazy stand,
Bare to the burning sky,
White-hot as glares the desert sand,
And dismal to the eye.
Its lid was like a rakish hat,
The tap bent all awry
And with a drip so constant that
It almost dripped when dry.
It was a most convenient tank
Wherein most things could fall;
Where snakes came from the bush and drank,
The rabbits used to call,
The mice committed suicide,
The gum leaves sank to rest,
And in it possums dropped and died
And hornets made their nest.
But stark within my memory
I see it once again
When we looked at it anxiously –
Days when we hoped for rain;
I hear the hollow sounds it made,
Like some prophetic drum,
As I tapped rung on rung, afraid
Of dreadful days to come.
When mother in despair would pray

As low the water sank:
Four rungs, three rungs, two rungs and, aye,
How miserly we drank;
And there was none for face or hands,
Waste was a wicked thing,
There in the baked and parching lands,
With hope our only spring.
Next came the fatal 'One rung left!'
(How cruel words can be!)
As we all stood of joys bereft,
Dumb in our misery:
And then I tapped the tank in pain –
Those knells of drought and doom:
Our tank at last gone dry again,
Our home cast down in gloom;
But, oh, the joy that filled our hearts
When came the bounteous rain
And the drain-pipe sang in fits and starts
And filled the tank again!

JAMES HACKSTON

From *A Song of Rain*

Mile on mile from Mallacoota
Runs the news, and far Baroota
Speeds it over hill and plain,
Till the slogan of the rain
Rolls afar to Yankalilla;
Wallaroo and Wirrawilla
Shout it o'er the leagues between,
Telling of the dawning green.
Frogs at Cocoroc are croaking,
Booboorowie soil is soaking,
Oodla Wirra, Orroroo
Breathe relief and hope anew.
Wycheproof and Wollongong
Catch the burden of the song
That is rolling, rolling ever
O'er the plains of Never Never
Sounding in each mountain rill,
Echoing from hill to hill. . .
In the lonely, silent places
Men lift up their glad, wet faces,
And their thanks ask no explaining –
It is raining – raining – raining!

C. J. DENNIS

Speaking of Cows

Speaking of cows
(Which no one was doing)
Why are they always
Staring and chewing?
Staring at people,
Chewing at clover,
Doing the same things
Over and over.

Once in a while,
You see a cow mooing,
Swishing her tail
At a fly that needs shooing.

Most of the time, though,
What's a cow doing?
Munching and looking,
Staring and chewing.
Eyes never blinking,
Jaws always moving.
What are cows thinking?
What are cows *proving?*

Cows mustn't care for
New Ways of doing.
That's what they stare for;
That's why they're chewing.

KAYE STARBIRD

43

In the Mountains on a Summer Day

Gently I stir a white feather fan,
With open shirt sitting in a green wood.
I take off my cap and hang it on a jutting stone;
A wind from the pine-tree trickles on my bare head.

LI PO (Translated from the Chinese by Arthur Waley)

Heat

The summer river:
although there is a bridge, my horse
goes through the water.

MASAOKA SHIKI

Biographies

Property of:
The John Bramston School
Witham, Essex

Tony Bradman is a writer and journalist. He has written several books for children, including the 'Dilly the Dinosaur' stories, and a book of verse, *Smile Please*. He lives in London with his wife and three children.

John Clare was born in 1793 in Northamptonshire, the son of a farm labourer. He taught himself, and became a successful writer while working as a labourer. He spent the last 23 years of his life in an asylum, and died there in 1864.

e. e. cummings (1894–1962) was a famous American poet. He experimented with typography and punctuation, often surprising the reader with the way the poem was laid out on the page. Some of his poems are very popular with children.

C. J. Dennis was born in South Australia in 1876. He had many jobs – solicitor's clerk, journalist, barman and odd-job man in the mines. He wrote *Songs of a Sentimental Bloke*, which was made into a television musical in 1976. He was resident poet for the *Melbourne Herald* newspaper until his death in 1936.

Emily Dickinson (1830–86) was one of the greatest American poets. She was very unlucky, because publishers thought her poems strange, and none was willing to publish them until after her death. Even then, publishers often changed her punctuation, and even altered some of the words she had written. She could say a great deal in a few short lines.

Lawrence Ferlinghetti was born in New York in 1920, and later moved to San Francisco. He has written many books of poetry, and was the proprietor of the famous City Lights bookshop. He has encouraged many young writers and published their books.

John Fuller was born in Kent in 1937. He has written several books for children, including a pantomime opera, 'The Spider Monkey Uncle King'. He is the son of the poet Roy Fuller.

Rebecca Gaskell was born in 1935 in the north of England, and writes poems for children and adults.

James Hackston (1888–1967) was the pen-name of Hal Gye. He was born in Australia. He illustrated C. J. Dennis's *Songs of a Sentimental Bloke*, and many other books. As James Hackston he wrote many short stories; he also had a third name, Hacko, which he used when writing light verse.

Ted Hughes was born in Yorkshire. In 1984 he was made Poet Laureate. He has written many books for adults and children. One of the best known for children is *Season Songs*, published by Faber and Faber.

Elizabeth Jennings was born in Lincolnshire in 1926. She worked as a library assistant before working in advertising and publishing. She has written many poems both for adults and children.

Rudyard Kipling was born in Bombay in 1865. He worked as a journalist and wrote his first poems and stories for newspapers and for the Indian Railway Library. He wrote many stories for children. After leaving India, he lived in Vermont, and then in Sussex, England, where he died in 1936. He was the first English writer to receive the Nobel Prize.

Li Po (701–761) was one of the greatest Chinese poets. He was born near present-day Afghanistan, and his family went to China when he was about five. He spent much of his life wandering, and is supposed to have died by falling out of a boat drunk, trying to 'embrace the moon in the river'.

A. A. Milne (1882–1956) must be one of the best-known names in this book. He wrote the famous Pooh stories for his son Christopher Robin, and his two books of poems for children – *When We Were Very Young* and *Now We Are Six* – are among the most popular collections of children's poems ever written.

James Reeves (1909–1978) was born near London. He wrote over 30 books, many of them books of poetry for children.

Carl Sandburg (1878–1967) was an American writer. After leaving school he wandered round Mid-West America, then went to fight in the Spanish-American war. He wrote many stories and poems for children, which are collected in *The Sandburg Treasury*.

Masaoka Shiki (1867–1902) was a Japanese writer of haiku. Shiki used to advise his pupils to be natural, and try for real pictures in their poems.

Index of first lines